About the B

The features of *Grammar and Punctuation, Grade 4* include:

25 Rule Charts

Reproduce these charts on overhead transparencies for ease of presentation.

Choose the rules and the order of use that are appropriate to the needs of your students.

Review the charts regularly.

3 Practice Pages for Each Rule

Use as many reproducible practice pages as appropriate for your students. These pages may be used with the whole class or as independent practice. You may wish to do a single practice page each time you review a rule.

Answer Key

A complete answer key begins on page 105.

About the CD-ROM

Loading the Program

1

Put the CD in your CD drive. This CD-ROM contains both Windows and MacOS programs.

Your computer will recognize the correct program.

2

On some computers, the program will automatically start up. If the program does not start automatically:

Windows—go to *My Computer*, double click on the CD drive, then double click on *Begin.exe*.

MacOS—double click on the CD icon on your desktop, then double click on *Begin*.

3

After the program starts, you will arrive at the main menu.

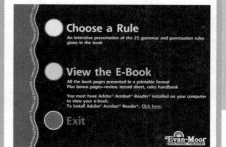

Main Menu Features

⬤ Choose a Rule

It's never been more fun to practice grammar and punctuation! The 25 rule charts found in the book are presented in full-color with an interactive element. To present a whole-class lesson, connect your computer to a projection system. As a review, students may be instructed on how to access specific rule charts during their computer time.

1
Click the *Choose a Rule* button to display the list of rules.

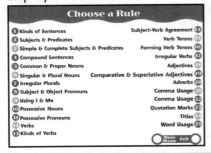

2
Click on a rule in the list of rules. The rule will be displayed.

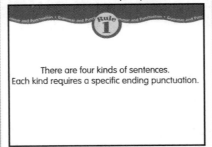

There are four kinds of sentences.
Each kind requires a specific ending punctuation.

3
Click on the arrow button.
Rule explanations and examples will be displayed.

4
When you're finished, click on 🔲 List of Rules ◯ to go back to the rules list or click on ◯ Main Menu to go back to the main menu.

⬤ View the E-Book

- The rule charts, practice pages, and answer key are presented in a printable electronic format. You must have Adobe® Acrobat® Reader™ installed to access the e-book. (See installation instructions in sidebar.)

- You may scroll through the entire book page by page or open the "Bookmarks" tab for a clickable table of contents.

  Hint: *This symbol, + for Windows or ▷ for MacOS, means that you can click there to expand this category.*

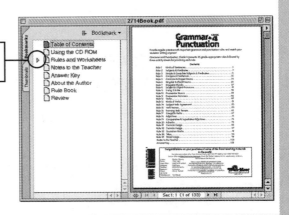

- To print pages from the e-book, click on the printer icon. A print dialog box will open. Enter the page or pages you wish to print in the print range boxes. (At the bottom of the screen, you can see which page of the e-book you are viewing.)

- To exit the e-box, simply "X" out until you return to the main menu.

E-Book Bonus

- Grammar and Punctuation Review
  This four-page review provides a means of evaluating your students' acquisition of the grammar and punctuation skills presented.

- Student Record Sheet
  On the student record sheet, the grammar and punctuation skills are keyed to the practice pages and the test items.

- Reproducible Rules Handbook
  Each rule is shown with room for students to write their own examples of the rule.

⬤ Exit

This button closes the program.

Installing Adobe® Acrobat® Reader™
You need to have Acrobat Reader installed on your computer to access the e-book portion of the CD-ROM. If you do not have Acrobat Reader, go to the main menu of the CD and follow these instructions:

1. Place your cursor over the *Click Here* link. Wait for the hand and then click.

2. When you see the Acrobat Reader Setup Screen, click the "Next" box.

3. When you see the Destination Location Screen, click the "Next" box.

4. When you see the Setup Complete Screen, click "finish."

Your system will now shut down in order to install Acrobat Reader. Some systems will automatically restart. If yours does not, start it up manually.

Rule 1

There are four kinds of sentences. Each kind requires a specific ending punctuation.

- A **declarative sentence** is a statement. It ends with a period (.).

    I heard a train whistle.

- An **interrogative sentence** asks a question. It ends with a question mark (**?**).

    Have you ever taken a train ride?

- An **imperative sentence** commands someone to do something. It ends with a period (.).

    Get on board the train now.

- An **exclamatory sentence** shows strong feeling. It ends with an exclamation mark (**!**).

    Watch out for that train!

Kinds of Sentences

Name _____

Kinds of Sentences

statement – tells something   •

question – asks something   ?

command – commands someone to do something   •

exclamation – shows strong feeling   !

A Add the correct punctuation at the end of each sentence. Then write the kind of sentence on the line.

1. What time do we catch the bus   _____

2. Let's meet at the park   _____

3. Don't leave your toys on the floor   _____

4. This is hard work   _____

5. Wow, what a surprise   _____

6. Mario and Karina went to Disneyland   _____

7. Can you help me fix this   _____

8. Put that away before you leave   _____

B Write one of each kind of sentence.

1. _____
statement

2. _____
question

3. _____
command

4. _____
exclamation

          Grammar and Punctuation, Grade 4 • EMC 2714

Name _____

Picture Sentences

Write a sentence to go with each picture. Write one **statement**, one **question**, one **command**, and one **exclamation**.

1.

_____

_____

_____

2.

_____

_____

_____

3.

_____

_____

_____

4.

_____

_____

_____

Write the Questions

Write a question to go with each answer below.

1. Adam made a big salad and set the table.

_____

_____

2. I am hoping to get a leather briefcase.

_____

_____

3. It happened when he was snowboarding at Big Mountain.

_____

_____

4. Jack's horse is the one with a white mane and tail.

_____

_____

5. He has two more years to go.

_____

_____

Rule 2

Every complete sentence has two parts.

- A **subject** names the person, place, or thing the sentence is about.

- A **predicate** tells what the subject is or does.

The hungry monkey *climbed a fruit tree*.
    subject   predicate

Disneyland *is a favorite vacation spot*.
    subject   predicate

Subjects & Predicates

Subject and Predicate Search

Rule 2

A Draw a line under the **subject** of each sentence. Draw a circle around the **predicate** of each sentence.

The stubborn donkey (stopped and sat down.)

1. The whole team cheered for their coach.

2. I feed my neighbor's cat.

3. The hungry children ate the leftover pizza.

4. Sally mowed the lawn after school.

5. Carlos receives his allowance every Friday.

B Write three complete sentences about your favorite animal. Draw a line under the subject of each sentence. Draw a circle around the predicate of each sentence.

1._____

_____

2._____

_____

3._____

_____

What's Missing?

Complete each sentence by filling in the missing subject or predicate.

1. The bus driver _____.

2. _____ enjoyed a picnic lunch.

3. _____ flew the plane safely.

4. Two bluebirds _____.

5. The famous chef _____.

6. _____ painted the fence for his grandma.

7. My teacher _____.

8. _____ ate all of the ice cream.

9. _____ watched a funny movie.

10. The carpenter _____.

Name _____

Sentence Search

Draw a circle around each complete sentence.

1. The kind police officer.

2. Three newborn kittens.

3. My friend Brenda helped me pack.

4. A shiny beetle crawled across the floor.

5. Went to the park.

6. Fell in the pool.

7. Found a five-dollar bill.

8. Sharon and her mother.

9. The puppy chewed on the shoe.

10. The owl at the top of that tree.

11. Sandy's Girl Scout troop went camping in the desert.

12. Her soft blue mittens.

13. Rose read a book.

14. We looked at the butterfly.

15. A family of foxes.

Use these rules to identify simple and complete subjects and predicates.

- The **complete subject** contains all the words that tell who or what the sentence is about.

- The **simple subject** is the main word or words in the complete subject.

simple subject

A funny clown did tricks.

complete subject

- The **complete predicate** contains all the words that tell what the subject is or does.

- The **simple predicate** is the main word or words in the complete predicate.

simple predicate

A deer jumped over the wall.

complete predicate

Simple & Complete Subjects & Predicates

Simple and Complete Subjects

Rule 3

A Draw a line under the **complete subject**. Write **SS** above the **simple subject**.

SS
The friendly librarian read a story to us.

1. My sister Amy gave me her old bike.

2. The large package was from Uncle Pete.

3. Several school bands marched in the parade.

4. George's pet dog caught the ball.

5. The frightened mouse ran behind the stove.

6. Everyone in the play did a good job.

B Write a **complete subject** using each of these words.

| lion | car | girl | pumpkin |

1. _____

2. _____

3. _____

4. _____

Simple and Complete Predicates

Rule 3

A Draw a line under the **complete predicate**. Write **SP** above the **simple predicate**.

SP
The raccoon ran down the trail.

1. My brother Ted gave me his old skates.

2. The largest giraffe ate from the top of the tree.

3. Many teams played in the baseball league.

4. Angela's pet hamster escaped from its cage.

5. The frightened puppy hid under Bob's bed.

6. We all helped wash the dirty car.

B Copy three complete predicates from sentences in a book. Write **SP** above the **simple predicate**.

1. _____

2. _____

3. _____

Subject and Predicate Match

Draw a line from the complete subject on the left to a complete predicate on the right to form a sentence that makes sense.

Our school's marching band   splashed in the mud and squealed.

Sixteen wild mustangs   organized the community softball game.

The courageous fire fighters   slept in the sunshine.

My little baby brother   jumped off a log and into the pond.

Rhonda's nephew Ray   performed the national anthem.

Mrs. Hamilton and Mr. Peters   galloped across the prairie.

The little pink pig   went on the field trip.

The whole class   cried when he lost his blanket.

A tired, old dog   rescued me from the burning building.

Two small green frogs   mowed the grass all by himself.

Rule 4

A compound sentence is made by putting two or more simple sentences together.

- The parts are usually joined by a conjunction such as **and**, **or**, or **but**.*

- A comma is placed before the conjunction.

Simple sentences:

He broke the window.
It was an accident.

Compound sentence:

*He broke the window, **but** it was an accident.*

Simple sentences:

I think I will eat a sandwich.
Maybe I'll have some pizza.

Compound sentence:

*I think I will eat a sandwich, **or** maybe I'll have some pizza.*

*See Notes to the Teacher on page 103 for additional information.

Compound Sentences

And, Or, But

A Circle the conjunctions in this paragraph.

> Mrs. Clark has an interesting job. She is a veterinarian, and she works in a zoo. She gives the animals medicine when they are sick, and she operates on them sometimes. She can clean their teeth, but she has to call a dentist to take care of bad teeth. Do you think you would like this job, or would you hate it?

B Write a sentence using each of these conjunctions.

and	or	but

1. _____

   _____

2. _____

   _____

3. _____

Name _____

Simple or Compound?

A A compound sentence is two or more simple sentences put together. Draw a line under the **simple sentences**. Draw a circle around the **compound sentences**.

The girl lost her bike.

Grandmother weeded the garden, and she planted new flowers.

1. We stacked the books on the librarian's desk.

2. The rain boots were stored in the closet, and the raincoats were hung in the hall.

3. My brother drank all of the milk, but he left some of the cookies.

4. Many people slipped on the icy sidewalk.

5. The referee blew his whistle at the end of the game.

6. I yelled at them to be careful, but it was too late.

B Now write a **simple sentence** about a kite, and write a **compound sentence** about a dinosaur.

1. _____

_____

2. _____

_____

Name _____

Write Compound Sentences

Use conjunctions (**and**, **or**, **but**) to join simple sentences together to make a compound sentence. Remember to add a comma before the conjunction in your sentences.

1. The children traded baseball cards.

Then they talked about the players.

_____

_____

2. The immigrants crossed the ocean.

Finally they reached a new land.

_____

_____

3. Do you want to go to the movies?

Would you rather go to the soccer game?

_____

_____

4. Eric wanted to go play ball with his friends.

He had to give the dog a bath first.

_____

_____

Rule 5

A noun names a person, place, or thing.

- **Common nouns** name any person, place, or thing. Common nouns do not begin with a capital letter.

  person—*teacher*   place—*park*   thing—*pinecone*

- **Proper nouns** name a specific person, place, or thing. Proper nouns begin with a capital letter.

common	proper
girl	Maria
town	Dallas
book	*Ramona, the Pest*
holiday	Arbor Day
river	Columbia River

Common & Proper Nouns

Find the Nouns

A Circle all the nouns in this list.

bake	long	Sally
school	bicycle	fuzzy
father	speak	park
curly	book	rough
carpenter	basket	feather
write	Jake	Marine World
hospital	reach	sleep
church	friend	pickle

B Write the nouns you circled in the correct category.

person	place	thing
_____	_____	_____
_____	_____	_____
_____	_____	_____
_____	_____	_____
_____	_____	_____

Name _____

Proper Nouns

A Rewrite the sentences and capitalize the proper nouns.

1. margo visited san francisco, california.

   _____

2. luis saw fireworks on the fourth of july.

   _____

3. columbus sailed across the atlantic ocean on the santa maria.

   _____

   _____

4. On august 14, dr. wang will begin working as a veterinarian at the san diego zoo.

   _____

   _____

B Write a proper noun for each of these.

your whole name _____

your school _____

your town _____

your favorite book _____

the country where you live _____

your best friend's name _____

Name _____

Correct the Capitalization

Rewrite the sentences. Capitalize the **proper** nouns. Draw a circle around the **common** nouns.

1. dr. green is my dentist.

_____

2. We ate kentucky fried chicken when rev. williams came to dinner.

_____

_____

3. juan garcia and maria montoya are in mr. martin's class.

_____

_____

4. My sister and I stayed with mr. and mrs. evans while our parents were in new york.

_____

_____

5. carl's birthday is on christmas day, but he celebrates it on december 26.

_____

_____

Rule 6

Singular nouns name one person, place, or thing. Plural nouns name more than one.

gorilla	jungle	watermelon
gorilla**s**	jungle**s**	watermelon**s**

- To make the plural of most nouns, add **s**.

    chair**s**   jacket**s**   orange**s**

- If the noun ends in *s, sh, ch, x,* or *z,* add **es**.

    bus**es**   dish**es**   bench**es**   box**es**

- If the noun ends in a consonant followed by a *y,* change the **y** to **i** and add **es**.

    baby—bab**ies**   story—stor**ies**   cherry—cherr**ies**

- If a noun ends in *f* or *fe,* add **s** to some; change **f** to **v** and add **es** to others.

    chief**s**   belief**s**   loa**ves**   lea**ves**

elf elves	shelf shelves	calf calves	*life lives
leaf leaves	loaf loaves	chiefs	
self selves	half halves	thief's	
	wolf wolves	*Knife Knives	

Singular & Plural Nouns

Noun Search

A Draw an **X** on the nouns that mean one (**singular**). Draw a box around the nouns that mean more than one (**plural**).

cats	guess	babies	bandage
cities	bus	foxes	berry
knives	vacation	tail	boxes
rabbit	benches	cliffs	cherries

B Write sentences using three of the **singular nouns**.

1. _____

2. _____

3. _____

C Write sentences using three of the **plural nouns**.

1. _____

2. _____

3. _____

Plural Nouns

A Rewrite these nouns to make them plural.

1. fox _____   6. cherry _____

2. puppy _____   7. guess _____

3. shelf _____   8. story _____

4. bush _____   9. ditch _____

5. toy _____   10. roof _____

B Write a sentence using the plural of each of these nouns.

1. berry

_____

_____

2. box

_____

_____

3. fence

_____

_____

Picture Plurals

A Write the singular noun for each of these pictures. Then write the plural form of the noun.

1.

singular _____

plural _____

2.

singular _____

plural _____

3.

singular _____

plural _____

4.

singular _____

plural _____

5.

singular _____

plural _____

6.

singular _____

plural _____

B Write one sentence using a singular noun and a plural noun.

_____

_____

Some nouns have special plural forms. They are called irregular plurals.

Singular	Irregular Plural
man	men
woman	women
goose	geese
child	children
foot	feet
mouse	mice
die	dice
ox	oxen

Irregular Plurals

Fill in the Blanks

A Change each singular noun to its plural form.

1. The _____ and _____ went to the party together.
   (man)   (woman)

2. Theresa has three _____ and five _____ for pets.
   (mouse)   (fish)

3. All the _____ and _____ were in the barn.
   (ox)   (goose)

4. Several _____ saw some _____ in the woods.
   (child)   (moose)

5. I wash my _____ and brush my _____ every day.
   (foot)   (tooth)

6. Those _____ are playing a game with two _____.
   (person)   (die)

B Look at a book or newspaper. List all of the irregular plural nouns you can find.

Plural Pathway

Rule 7

Color a path through the grid from "start" to "finish" by using only the boxes that contain plural nouns. You may move up, down, left or right, but NOT diagonally. Hint: Be sure to watch for irregular plurals!

 start

children	hero	cheese	gentlemen	wishes	men
dice	base	dress	socks	nose	donkeys
deer	shoes	rash	giants	size	libraries
kiss	people	mind	women	guest	dishes
grape	houses	thimble	babies	city	teeth
mess	mice	oxen	bees	gas	feet

 finish

Name _____

An Irregular Story

A Write the plural form of each of these nouns.

1. foot _____

2. child _____

3. person _____

4. mouse _____

5. tooth _____

6. goose _____

7. woman _____

8. man _____

B Write a story using at least four of the irregular plurals above.

_____

_____

_____

_____

_____

_____

_____

C Draw a picture to illustrate your story.

Rule 8

A pronoun is used in the place of a noun.

- A **subject pronoun** replaces a noun used as the subject of a sentence.

I	you	he	she	they	it

Mark wanted to ride the horse.
He wanted to ride the horse.

Sean and James went to camp last summer.
They went to camp last summer.

- An **object pronoun** replaces a noun used after an action verb.*

me	you	him	her	it	us	them

Sarah will meet _Jake_ at noon.
Sarah will meet **him** at noon.

Clarissa went with _Mindy and Jo_ to the circus.
Clarissa went with **them** to the circus.

*See Notes to the Teacher on page 103 for additional information.

Subject & Object Pronouns

Change Nouns to Pronouns

Write a pronoun for each of the underlined words or phrases in these sentences.

1. <u>Terri</u> asked <u>Dad</u> to pass <u>the potatoes</u>.

_____

_____

2. <u>Sue and Mary</u> took <u>the puppy</u> on the trip.

_____

_____

3. <u>The zoo ranger</u> won't let us feed <u>the wild animals</u>.

_____

_____

4. <u>Tom and I</u> painted <u>the fence</u> quickly.

_____

_____

5. Why are <u>Lee and Stella</u> cutting <u>the bush</u> in the backyard?

_____

_____

6. <u>Carlos</u> lent <u>his basketball</u> to <u>Roberto and me</u>.

_____

_____

Use the Correct Word

A Write **we** or **us** in each blank.

1. May _____ make some popcorn?

2. Is it time for _____ to go home?

3. It was fun for _____ to sleep in the tent.

4. _____ have a new puppy.

B Write **they** or **them** in each blank.

1. Is the package for _____?

2. We went to school with _____.

3. We will eat dinner when _____ are ready.

4. _____ are moving to Dallas.

C Write sentences using each of these pronouns.

we	us	they	them

1. _____

2. _____

3. _____

4. _____

Name _____

Picture Pronouns

A Label each picture with a pronoun.

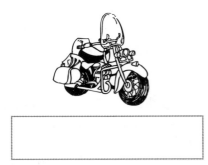

B Write a sentence about each picture. Be sure to use at least one pronoun in each sentence.

1. _____

_____

2. _____

_____

3. _____

_____

4. _____

_____

Name yourself last when you are talking about another person and yourself.

*Roberto and **I** ran around the track.*
*The coach and **I** sat together on the bus.*

*Did you see Jim and **me** swim across the lake?*
*Maria takes ballet lessons with Tanya and **me**.*

- To hear if you used **I** or **me** correctly, leave out the other person's name.

  Which would you say?

  *Roberto and **I** ran around the track.*
  *(**I** ran around the track.)*

  *Roberto and **me** ran around the track.*
  *(**Me** ran around the track.)*

  *Maria takes ballet lessons with Tanya and **me**.*
  *(Maria takes ballet lessons with **me**.)*

  *Maria takes ballet lessons with Tanya and **I**.*
  *(Maria takes ballet lessons with **I**.)*

Using I & Me

I or Me?

A Write **I** or **me** in each blank.

1. Jenny and _____ like to ice-skate.

2. Pete wants my sister and _____ to come to a barbecue at his house.

3. Maurice and _____ like to write stories together.

4. My mother and _____ have to go to the dentist this afternoon.

5. Will you help Phil and _____ fix the flat tire on my bike?

6. The farmer let Annie and _____ ride the pony.

7. Most of my friends like to play football, but Toni and _____ like to play soccer.

8. Carlos, can you come with my cousin and _____ to the fair Saturday afternoon?

B Write two sentences about something you and one of your friends like to do.
Use the word **I** in one sentence and **me** in the other.

1. _____

_____

2. _____

_____

Name _____

All About Me

A Circle the sentences that use **I** or **me** correctly.

1. Mother helped my friends and me bake some cookies.

2. I and Robin counted the eggs.

3. My mother cracked the eggs into a bowl for Robin and me.

4. I and Kevin measured the flour.

5. Cory and I poured the flour into the bowl.

6. Alicia melted the butter for Petra and me.

7. Timo and I added the chocolate chips to the batter.

8. Petra put the pans in the sink for me and Kevin to wash.

B Write a sentence about your favorite kind of cookie. Use a friend's name and the word **I** or **me** in your sentence.

_____

_____

C Draw a picture of your favorite kind of cookie.

Find the Mistakes

A Circle the words that are used incorrectly. The first one has been done for you.

Meg, Jane, and me went to the fair. Jane and me went on all the rides.

Then we looked at the farm animals. Meg liked the baby pigs, but me and

Jane thought the goats were cuter. Meg bought some corn on the cob for

Jane and I to eat. We were still hungry, so Jane bought ice-cream cones

for Meg and I. After dark, Jane and me watched the amazing fireworks

show.

B Rewrite the paragraph on the lines below, using the words correctly. Write a concluding sentence for the paragraph.

_____

_____

_____

_____

_____

_____

_____

Rule 10

A possessive noun shows ownership.

- To make a **singular** noun show ownership, add an apostrophe (') and **s**.

  *Arturo**'s** football*

  *the police officer**'s** hat*

  *James**'s** bicycle*

- To make a **plural** noun that ends in *s* show ownership, just add an apostrophe (').

  *the sister**s'** slumber party*

  *our team**s'** uniforms*

  *the puppie**s'** leashes*

- To make a **plural** noun that does not end in *s* show ownership, add an apostrophe (') and **s**.

  *the women**'s** dresses*

  *the mice**'s** nests*

  *the children**'s** toys*

Possessive Nouns

Who Owns It?

A Write the possessive form of each noun.

singular—'s   plural—s'

1. two _____ sweaters
   (girls)

2. my _____ collar
   (dog)

3. several _____ cookbooks
   (mothers)

4. the _____ cage
   (bunny)

5. those _____ tools
   (workers)

6. both _____ game
   (boys)

7. the _____ instruments
   (band)

8. _____ birthday
   (Kate)

B Make a label using your name to show that you own something.

> This is _____.
>   (possessive form of your name)

Name _____

Fairy Tale Fun

A Fill in the blanks with possessive nouns from familiar fairy tales.

1. Goldilocks ate the _____ porridge.

2. Jack climbed the beanstalk and stole the _____ treasures.

3. The three Billy Goats Gruff crossed over the _____ bridge.

4. The big, bad wolf blew down the little _____ houses.

5. Red Riding Hood walked to her _____ home in the forest.

6. _____ fairy godmother turned a pumpkin into a coach.

7. Hansel and Gretel nibbled on the _____ gingerbread house.

8. Everyone pretended that they could see the _____ new clothes.

B Draw a picture to illustrate your favorite fairy tale.

Name _____

Possessives That Rhyme

Draw a line from each name to the object that rhymes with it.

1.

2.

3.

4.

5.

6.

7.

8.

Write each rhyming possessive.

1. _Rick's stick_

2. _____

3. _____

4. _____

5. _____

6. _____

7. _____

8. _____

   42 Grammar and Punctuation, Grade 4 • EMC 2714

Rule 11

Possessive pronouns show ownership. They replace possessive nouns.

There are two kinds of possessive pronouns. They do not require an apostrophe.

• One kind is used before a noun.

my	your	his	her	its	our	their

our home   ***her*** brother   ***my*** best friend

• The second type stands alone.

mine	yours	his	hers	its	ours	theirs

*Is this book **yours**?*   *Yes, it is **mine**.*

Possessive Pronouns

Fill in the Blanks

A Write a possessive pronoun in each blank to complete the sentences.

| my | mine | our | his | her | its | their | your |

1. Tom rode _____ horse along the trail.

2. The boys can't find _____ homework.

3. "When do you have to go home?" Sue asked _____ friend.

4. _____ friends went on a trip with us.

5. "When will _____ work be done?" Mr. Lee asked Fred.

6. The dog ate _____ bone.

7. I feed _____ fish every day.

8. He asked me if the pencils are _____.

B Write a sentence using each of these possessive pronouns.

| my | our | their |

1. _____

2. _____

3. _____

Name _____

Pick a Possessive Pronoun

Write the pronoun that makes the most sense in each sentence.

1. Madge and Joe played with _____ cousins at the family reunion.
(its   their   your)

2. The droopy dog lazily scratched at _____ fleas.
(my   our   its)

3. Rosie received many gifts at _____ going-away party.
(your   his   her)

4. Gabriel started _____ new job today.
(their   our   his)

5. These pesky ants are looking for food to take back to _____ colony.
(our   their   your)

6. Emily fell and hurt _____ knee quite seriously.
(her   his   my)

7. Only you can control _____ own behavior.
(my   its   your)

8. When Tim and I found a leak in _____ canoe, we paddled faster than ever.
(your   our   its)

Name _____

Fractured Sentences

Use one phrase from each column to build a complete sentence. Write your sentences on the lines below. Be sure all of your sentences make sense!

column a	column b	column c
Serena found	his finger	in the closet.
I wrote	their food	from a bowl.
Randall and I whispered	its frisbee	quietly.
Avery cut	your saxophone	in the air.
The cats ate	my story	beautifully.
You played	her hat	with a pocketknife.
The dog caught	our secrets	about birds.

1. _____

2. _____

3. _____

4. _____

5. _____

6. _____

7. _____

Rule 12

A verb is a word in the predicate that tells action or state of being.

He **ran** down the road.

They **played** for our team.

Mark **laughed** at the joke.

I **went** to town.

Sarah **was** sad.

Verbs

Verb Hunt

A Read this story. Draw a circle around all the verbs.

> My friend Tony and I went to the beach yesterday. We climbed on the
> rocks and built castles in the sand.
>
> We saw interesting plants and animals in the tide pools. Tony picked up
> a crab, but he yelled and dropped it fast. The crab pinched his finger!
>
> I stood too close to the waves. Tony yelled, "Look out!" It was too late. I
> was soaked. Tony laughed so hard he fell down. I will be more careful next time.

B Now write your own paragraph telling about something you did yesterday. When
you are finished, circle all the verbs you used.

_____

_____

_____

_____

_____

_____

_____

_____

Name _____

Choose a Verb

A Write a verb in each blank to complete the sentences.

1. Jeremy _____ to the other side of the pool.

2. The car _____ at the signal.

3. Mr. Taylor _____ the children a new song.

4. Our team _____ the championship game.

5. Albert _____ to the band at the concert.

6. The eagle _____ over the fields.

B Write a sentence using each of these verbs.

| stumbled | became | reached | think |

1. _____

_____

2. _____

_____

3. _____

_____

4. _____

_____

Verb Categories

A Write each verb below under the name of the animal that is most likely to do the action it describes. Use a dictionary if you need help.

slither	bask	soar	buzz
gallop	scream	whinny	sting
canter	coil	flit	dive

bee	horse	snake	eagle

B What is your favorite animal?

_____

Write three verbs that describe actions done by this animal.

_____

_____

_____

Rule 13

There are three kinds of verbs.

- **Action verbs** tell what the subject is doing.

    *He **played** quarterback all season.*

    *Margo **sang** in the school choir.*

- **Linking verbs** link a subject to a noun or an adjective that names or describes it.

    *His bike **is** red with blue trim.*

    *The clown **looked** funny in his big shoes.*

- **Helping verbs** come before the main verb. They help state the action or show time.

    *Carlos **will** clean up the backyard.*

    *Tamera **has been** sewing this afternoon.*

Kinds of Verbs

Verbs on the Move

Find all the actions that are taking place in this picture. Write the verbs that describe those actions on the lines.

_____

_____

_____

_____

_____

_____

_____

_____

Name _____

Linking Verbs

A Circle the linking verb in each sentence.

1. Richard was the referee at the boxing match.

2. Mrs. Murphy became a teacher in September.

3. The chocolate cake tasted delicious.

4. Tomorrow is my birthday.

5. The speakers were entertaining.

6. I am tired.

7. The weather is too cold for me.

8. The trail looks treacherous.

B Write a sentence using each of these linking verbs.

| smells | seemed | feel |

1. _____

2. _____

3. _____

Helping Verbs

A Underline the **action verb** in each sentence. Then circle the **helping verb**.

The puppy (has been) wagging its tail all day.

1. Ms. Smith had baked cookies for the party.

2. My dad has been reading a story about pirates to us.

3. Pretty butterflies are flying around the flowers.

4. The soccer team had won all of its games this year.

5. We have finished our homework.

6. Mother was working this morning.

B Write a sentence using each of these helping verbs.

| is | have | had | are | was | were |

1. _____

2. _____

3. _____

4. _____

5. _____

6. _____

Rule 14

The verb in a sentence must agree with the subject of the sentence.

- If the subject is singular, the verb must also be singular.

  Mario **sings** _in the school chorus._

  The _baby_ **is** _crying._

- If the subject is plural, the verb must also be plural.

  Mario and his brothers **sing** _in the school chorus._

  The _babies_ **are** _crying._

Subject-Verb Agreement

Name _____

Choose the Correct Verb

A Circle the correct verb to complete each sentence.

1. They (play   plays) the game carefully.

2. Mystery stories (is   are) exciting.

3. Ms. Trent (paint   paints) murals on buildings.

4. My kite (fly   flies) over the tops of the trees.

5. The robin (lay   lays) blue eggs in her nest.

6. The girls (dance   dances) beautifully.

B Write sentences using each of these subjects.

tigers   the scientist   helicopter   flowers

1. _____

_____

2. _____

_____

3. _____

_____

4. _____

_____

Match Subjects and Verbs

A Match each subject on the left with the verb form on the right that agrees.

1. Sara	rings
2. Robins	plan
3. The books	purrs
4. He and Bob	paints
5. The boats	fly
6. Teachers	are
7. The phone	sail
8. My cat	run

B Write complete sentences using the matching subjects and verbs above.

1. _____

2. _____

3. _____

4. _____

5. _____

6. _____

7. _____

8. _____

Name _____

Is, Are, Has, Have

Write one of the words below in each blank. Be sure the sentences make sense.

is	are	has	have

1. The ponies _____ eating hay.

2. My brother _____ working in the barn.

3. The baby goats _____ sleeping.

4. The mother hen _____ six eggs in her nest.

5. Some of the cows _____ horns.

6. Our four woolly sheep _____ grazing in the meadow.

7. Grandpa's horse _____ a soft nose.

8. Billy's rabbit _____ fond of carrots.

9. The children all _____ chores to do.

10. Our neighbor _____ a flock of geese.

Rule 15

The tense of a verb tells when an action occurs— present, past, or future.

- **present**—the action is happening now.

    *Tomas **is playing** tennis with Billy.*

    *Lee **runs** to catch the bus.*

    *I **buy** stamps at the post office.*

- **past**—the action already happened.

    *Tomas **played** tennis with George yesterday.*

    *Lee **ran** to catch the bus.*

    *I **bought** stamps at the post office.*

- **future**—the action is going to happen.

    *Tomas **will play** tennis with Allen next Saturday.*

    *Lee **will run** to catch the bus.*

    *I **shall buy** stamps at the post office tomorrow.*

Verb Tenses

When Did It Happen?

Rule
15

Label each sentence **past**, **present**, or **future** to tell when the action in the sentence takes place.

1. The tired nurse sat down to rest.   _____

2. Pete throws the ball for his dog Bingo to catch.   _____

3. Tomorrow I will study for my test.   _____

4. June and Lara will travel to India next month.   _____

5. The boys forgot to pick up their wet towels.   _____

6. Ray reads his newspaper.   _____

7. Aunt Helen made a gorgeous cake for my last birthday. _____

8. Mr. Burton will work on the tree house on Saturday.   _____

9. The hamburgers we ate for dinner were very good.   _____

10. Tim is happy.   _____

Use Verb Tenses

A Complete these sentences using a present tense verb.

1. My horse _____ .

2. All of the children _____ .

3. Mrs. Hallifax _____ .

4. His new jacket _____ .

B Complete these sentences using a past tense verb.

1. Yesterday I _____ .

2. Our lunch _____ .

3. Christopher _____ .

4. The librarian _____ .

C Complete these sentences using a future tense verb.

1. The teenage boys _____ .

2. Molly and Peggy _____ .

3. The monster _____ .

4. Our teacher _____ .

Verb Tense Categories

Rule
15

Write each verb or verb phrase below under the correct heading.

sings	jokes	shall speak
thought	speaks	climbed
will send	will plant	tastes
will buy	fell	shall make
removed	enjoys	lost

past	present	future

Rule 16

Endings are added to verbs to change the tense.

Present

- add **s** to most verbs*   *swings*
- add **ing** and use a present tense helping verb   *is swinging*
- verbs ending in *s*, *ch*, *sh*, *x*, or *z*—add **es**   *catches*
- verbs ending in *y*—change **y** to **i** and add **es**   *cries*

Past

- add **ed** to most verbs   *worked*
- add **ing** and use a past tense helping verb   *was working*
- verbs ending in a single vowel and consonant—   *skipped*
  double the final consonant and add **ed**
- verbs ending in *e*—drop the **e** and add **ed**   *placed*
- verbs ending in *y*—change **y** to **i** and add **ed**   *carried*

Future

- use the main verb with **will** or **shall**   ***will*** *dance*

                                                                                   shall *come*

*See Notes to the Teacher on page 103 for additional information.

Forming Verb Tenses

Present Tense Verbs

To make present tense verbs:
- add **s** to most verbs
- when a verb ends in *s*, *sh*, *ch*, *x*, or *z*—add **es**
- when a verb ends in *y*—change the **y** to **i** and add **es**

A Write the present tense of each verb by adding **s**, **es**, or **ies**.

1. bake   _____

2. hurry   _____

3. try   _____

4. reach   _____

5. cry   _____

6. rush   _____

7. fry   _____

8. wash   _____

9. mix   _____

10. pass   _____

11. play   _____

12. buzz   _____

B Use the verbs above to complete each sentence.

1. The baby _____ when she is hungry.

2. Ms. Cohen _____ our house every day on her way to work.

3. He _____ to catch the bus.

4. Dad _____ the car every Saturday afternoon.

5. This Friday our team _____ the Blue Hornets.

6. Uncle Ed _____ the best apple pie.

Past, Present, or Future?

Rule 16

A Write the correct verb tense in each sentence.

1. We _____ football yesterday afternoon.
   (play)

2. My dog can _____ over that high fence.
   (jump)

3. Before he went to work, Mr. Brown _____ around the park three times.
   (jog)

4. Can you see where the snail _____ on the flower?
   (nibble)

5. Please _____ past the sleeping baby's room.
   (tiptoe)

6. The shy child _____ when he is ready.
   (speak)

7. Mr. Pak _____ the flag every morning.
   (raise)

8. We _____ the Grand Canyon next summer.
   (visit)

B Write three sentences using the word *walk*. Use a different tense for each sentence.

1. _____

2. _____

3. _____

It Already Happened

A Write **past** or **present** on the line after each verb.

1. listened _____

2. raised _____

3. stopped _____

4. visit _____

5. creaked _____

6. leap _____

7. cried _____

8. crossed _____

9. approach _____

10. skipped _____

B Write the past tense of these verbs.

1. flip _____

2. agree _____

3. carry _____

4. row _____

5. watch _____

6. tag _____

7. drop _____

8. try _____

9. admire _____

10. hurry _____

Some verbs do not follow a set rule to form the past tense. These verbs are called irregular verbs.

Present	Past
swim	swam
bring	brought
know	knew
come	came
have	had
do	did
say	said
see	saw
sing	sang
write	wrote
is	was
are	were
give	gave
buy	bought
begin	began

Irregular Verbs

Match Verb Forms

Match each verb on the left to its past tense form on the right.

blow	drank
rise	came
choose	swam
freeze	took
steal	felt
break	fought
think	rose
feel	wore
throw	froze
wear	chose
speak	threw
grow	grew
take	stole
fight	spoke
drink	blew
swim	broke
come	thought

Use Irregular Verbs

Fill in each blank with the past tense form of each irregular verb.

1. Tammy's heart _____ when she heard the bad news.
(sink)

2. Gary _____ an award at the ceremony last week.
(win)

3. Dan _____ to bring his homework to school.
(forget)

4. Alex _____ a gigantic soap bubble.
(blow)

5. Ryan _____ a dollar bill on the sidewalk.
(find)

6. When Alice was a little girl, she _____ dresses to school.
(wear)

7. Mr. Jennings _____ pizza to our class party.
(bring)

8. The kittens _____ through the night.
(sleep)

9. Our family _____ the whole turkey in one sitting.
(eat)

10. The bus driver _____ carefully on the icy road.
(drive)

Word Search

A Circle the 18 irregular verbs hidden in this word search. Look up, down, left, right, and diagonally. The first one has been done for you.

```
f   b   d   c   a   t   c   h   f   g   t
r   h   k   a   e   p   s   o   v   n   a
e   l   e   a   v   e   j   l   g   i   v
e   e   m   w   i   n   p   d   s   r   l
z   s   f   i   n   d   s   e   e   b   e
e   o   c   g   e   r   i   s   e   w   e
g   o   k   i   l   r   k   e   e   p   f
a   h   b   v   d   w   a   r   d   o   m
r   c   n   e   k   a   t   p   y   u   b
```

B Write the irregular verbs on the lines. Then write the past tense form of each irregular verb.

freeze	froze	
_____	_____	_____ _____
_____	_____	_____ _____
_____	_____	_____ _____
_____	_____	_____ _____
_____	_____	_____ _____
_____	_____	_____ _____
_____	_____	_____ _____

Rule 18

Adjectives describe nouns or pronouns.

Adjectives can tell three things:

- **what kind**

    The **small** kitten climbed that **tall** tree.

    Beautiful white clouds blew across the sky.

- **which one**

    This soccer ball is mine.

    I ate two of **those** cookies.

- **how many**

    Some birds migrate south in the winter.

    The **two** buildings have **many** windows.

Adjectives

Name _____

Describe It

Rewrite each sentence by adding adjectives to describe the underlined nouns.

1. The <u>lion</u> chased the <u>zebra</u>.

_____

_____

2. The <u>street</u> was filled with <u>cars</u> and <u>buses</u>.

_____

_____

3. The <u>woman</u> sat on the <u>bench</u> to rest.

_____

_____

4. Carrie ate <u>apples</u> and drank <u>lemonade</u>.

_____

_____

5. The <u>boy</u> won a <u>bike</u> in a contest.

_____

_____

Name _____

Adjective Pictures

Draw a picture to show the meaning of the adjectives in each phrase. Use a dictionary if you need help.

a drowsy cat	the irate old man
a scarlet blossom	the ferocious beast
a symmetrical pattern	the gleeful winner

Name _____

Find a Path

Color a path through the grid from "start" to "finish" by using only the boxes that contain adjectives. You may move up, down, left or right, but NOT diagonally.

 **start**

soft	sour	delicious	purple	simple	strong
mushroom	jacket	building	resort	helicopter	busy
chapter	towel	ignite	sweet	tired	blue
nephew	introduce	pencil	small	sofa	paper
polish	respond	shoe	hard	enormous	cold
citizen	hobby	parachute	sleep	automobile	grouchy

 **finish**

Rule 19

Adjectives can make comparisons.

- Use **er** to compare two people, places, or things.

  *Tony is a **faster** runner than Jamal.*

  *This is the **sharper** of the two pencils.*

  *Who is **shorter**, Terri or Michael?*

- Use **est** to compare three or more people, places, or things.

  *He is the **fastest** runner in school.*

  *Of the three girls, she has the **longest** hair.*

  *That was the **greatest** story I've ever heard!*

Comparative & Superlative Adjectives

Make Comparisons

A Write the correct adjective in each sentence. Add the ending **er** or **est**.

1. She is _____ than Marsha.
   (strong)

2. Who is the _____ person in your class?
   (smart)

3. Mr. Gonzales is the _____ person in our town.
   (old)

4. I worked _____ today than yesterday.
   (hard)

5. My jacket is _____ than my sweater.
   (warm)

6. Ms. Davis is the _____ person I know.
   (kind)

B Write two sentences. Use **slower** in one sentence and **slowest** in the other sentence.

1. _____

   _____

2. _____

   _____

Name _____

Bigger, Taller, Faster

Circle the correct object in each picture. Then write a sentence comparing the two objects.

Which is **longer**?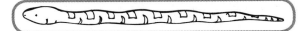

*The snake is **longer** than the caterpillar.*

1. Which is **bigger**?

_____

2. Which is **hotter**?

_____

3. Which is **softer**?

_____

4. Which is **taller**?

_____

5. Which is **faster**?

_____

Name _____

Super Sentences

Fill in each blank with an adjective. Use an **er** or **est** ending. Be sure that the word you choose makes sense in the sentence.

1. The peacock's feathers are _____ than the emu's feathers.

2. Margaret was the _____ girl in her family.

3. Sequoia trees are the _____ trees in the world.

4. Janet wears _____ shoes than I do.

5. The clown in the polka dot pants is _____ than the other one.

6. My brown dog is _____ than my little black puppy.

7. Mrs. Everett says that our class is the _____ class in the school.

8. Grandfather drives the _____ car I have ever seen.

9. Sparky is the _____ horse in the stable.

10. George was the _____ fire fighter at the station.

Rule 20

An adverb is a word that describes a verb, an adjective, or another adverb.

- Adverbs can tell

  how: *The mouse scampered **quickly** into the hole.*

  where: *A pine tree is growing **there** in the garden.*

  when: *The baby is smiling happily **now**.*

  to what extent: *That cocoa is **very** hot.*

- Here are some common adverbs.

how	where	when	to what extent
quickly	there	now	very
honestly	here	never	quite
suddenly	everywhere	soon	too
happily	away	yesterday	extremely

Adverbs

Find the Adverb

Rule 20

A Draw a circle around the adverb that tells about the underlined verb.

1. Annie <u>sang</u> quietly to her little sister.

2. Carlos <u>played</u> over there.

3. Please <u>ride</u> carefully.

4. Cereal <u>flew</u> everywhere when I dropped the box.

5. The doctor <u>waited</u> patiently for the test results.

6. His dog <u>wiggled</u> nervously at bathtime.

B Write a sentence using an adverb that tells **how**.

_____

_____

C Write a sentence using an adverb that tells **where**.

_____

_____

D Write a sentence using an adverb that tells **when**.

_____

_____

Name _____

How? When? Where?

A Draw a circle around each adverb.

1. They searched carefully.

2. They searched everywhere.

3. They are searching now.

4. The children played nearby.

5. The children played yesterday.

6. The children played quietly.

7. The neighbors returned quickly.

8. The neighbors returned early.

9. The neighbors returned home.

B Write each adverb that you circled under the correct heading.

how	when	where
_____	_____	_____
_____	_____	_____
_____	_____	_____

Verbs and Adverbs

A Draw a line under each **verb**. Draw a circle around each **adverb**.

1. The little boy played carefully with the tiny puppy.

2. The kind clerk cheerfully helped the customer.

3. James worked quickly to finish his homework.

4. The sleepy bear growled angrily.

5. The large audience clapped loudly.

6. Mr. Yi plays the piano often.

7. Sarah whispered quietly to her best friend.

B Rewrite each sentence. Add an adverb.

1. The firefly flew away.

   _____

2. Jack bounced the ball.

   _____

3. The band played music.

   _____

4. My neighbor planted flowers in his garden.

   _____

Rule 21

Use these rules for commas in dates, addresses, and letters.

- to separate the day and year in a date.*

  January 1, 2002

  November 12, 1945

- to separate a city and state, province, or country.*

  Memphis, Tennessee

  Calgary, Alberta

- after the greeting in a friendly letter.

  Dear Aunt Martha,

  Dear Joey and Carlos,

- after the closing in a letter.

  Sincerely,

  Your friend,

*See Notes to the Teacher on page 103 for additional information.

Comma Usage

Dates and Addresses

Rule
21

Rewrite each sentence. Add commas where they are needed.

1. On April 9 1942 my grandfather was inducted into the U.S. Army.

_____

_____

2. The Melvin family visited Vancouver British Columbia on their vacation.

_____

_____

3. The new school in Mesa Arizona will open on September 15 2002.

_____

_____

4. The Empire State Building is located in New York New York.

_____

_____

5. Emily Rogers moved from Nashville Tennessee to Seattle Washington.

_____

_____

Friendly Letters

Copy the letters. Add commas where they are needed.

Dear Beverly

I am now a counselor at Camp Wildwood. It is a fabulous camp near Boise Idaho. I started work on June 9 2001. I am having lots of fun.

> Your best friend
>
> Paulette

_____

_____

_____

_____

Dear Paulette

Your job sounds wonderful. I will be traveling this summer. I am going to Paris France and London England. I leave on July 6 2001. I can't wait!

> Yours truly
>
> Beverly

_____

_____

_____

_____

Name _____

Write a Letter

Write a letter to a friend telling about a real or imagined event in your life. Be sure to use commas correctly.

_____

_____

_____

_____

_____

_____

_____

_____

_____

_____

Rule 22

Commas are used in specific instances.

- to separate three or more words or phrases in a series.

  I have my umbrella, raincoat, and boots ready.

  They rode over the bridge, down the road, and into the barn.

- after introductory words such as *yes*, *no*, and *well*.

  Yes, you may have dessert now.

  Well, I never heard that before!

- to set off the name of a person being spoken to from the rest of the sentence.

  Clarence, can you help me lift this?

  Come here, Patricia, and help me.

Comma Usage

Commas in a Series

A Add commas between three or more items that come in a series.

1. We went to the movies with Careen Paul and Maria.

2. Mrs. Clancy planted roses tulips zinnias and carnations in her flower garden.

3. We ate sandwiches potato chips and cookies at the picnic.

4. Snakes fish and turtles all have scales.

5. Did you go to Disneyland Magic Mountain or Marine World on your vacation?

6. The children ran on the beach waded in the water and built sand castles.

7. Mosquitoes crickets and owls kept the campers awake most of the night.

8. Lightning flashed thunder roared and gusty winds blew during the storm.

B Write a sentence using three or more words in a series.

_____

_____

_____

Name _____

Use Commas

Complete these sentences. Don't forget the commas.

1. Yes_____

_____

2. No _____

_____

3. Well _____

_____

4. Mr. Doolittle_____

_____

5. Sam _____

_____

6. Anita _____

_____

A Conversation

A Fill in the blanks to complete this conversation. Be sure to add commas where they are needed.

"Rudy may I borrow your _____."

"No Alex you may not."

"Well why won't you let me?"

"Because Alex the last time you borrowed it _____."

"Gee Rudy I promise _____."

"Okay Alex you may borrow my _____. But please

_____."

B Draw a picture to illustrate the conversation.

Rule 23

A quotation is the exact words a person says.

A quotation:	Not a quotation:
"I will go to the grocery store," said Mandy.	*Mandy said that she would go to the grocery store.*

- **Quotation marks** (" ") are placed before and after a speaker's exact words.*

  "My birthday is coming," said Amy. "Can you come to my party?"

  "I will have to ask my parents," answered Marcus.

- The first word inside the quotation marks begins with a capital letter.

  *Aaron stated, "**W**e found those rocks beside the stream."*

  *"**W**hat are you doing?" questioned Tomas. "**I**t sounds like something broke."*

*See Notes to the Teacher on page 103 for additional information.

Quotation Marks

What Did You Say?

A Rewrite each sentence. Add quotation marks to show each person's exact words.

1. Maggie said, I'll get us something to eat.

   _____

2. Do you have any brothers? asked Bill.

   _____

3. Beth shouted, Keep away from that fire!

   _____

4. Why do I always have to take out the garbage? complained Chris.

   _____

5. Willie said, I want to be a veterinarian when I grow up.

   _____

6. The game will start in a few minutes, announced the coach.

   _____

B Write a sentence using quotation marks to show what someone is saying.

_____

_____

_____

_____

Put It in Quotes

Rule 23

Change each sentence to a direct quotation. Be sure to use quotation marks.

Randy said that he enjoyed the dinner.
"I enjoyed the dinner," said Randy.

1. Leonard said that the class party starts at two o'clock.

_____

_____

2. Fran told us that she saw an accident on the highway.

_____

_____

3. Marcus mentioned that Sam and Shirley are both in the play.

_____

_____

4. Our teacher explained that there would be a lunar eclipse tonight.

_____

_____

5. Mr. Jennings reminded me that we have a science test tomorrow.

_____

_____

Write a Dialogue

A Write an imaginary conversation between yourself and a parent. In the conversation, you are asking your parent's permission to get a pet. Be sure to use quotation marks.

_____

_____

_____

_____

_____

_____

_____

_____

_____

_____

B Draw a picture of the kind of pet you would most like to get.

Rule 24

Titles of books, movies, plays, magazines, songs, stories, etc., are treated in specific ways.

- Capitalize the first word, the last word, and every important word in between.*

  ***S**aint **G**eorge and the **D**ragon*

  ***S**tories from the **S**ilk **R**oad*

  ***M**y **A**dventures in the **D**eep*

- When you write in handwriting, underline the titles of books, movies, and television programs, and the names of newspapers and magazines.

  <u>Wheel of Fortune</u> (television show)

  <u>Horton Hears a Who</u> (book)

- If you are using a word processor, use italics instead of underlining.

  Wheel of Fortune (television show)

  Horton Hears a Who (book)

- Use quotation marks around the titles of stories, magazine articles, essays, songs, and most poems.

  "America the Beautiful" (song)

  "Pecos Bill and the Tornado" (story)

*See Notes to the Teacher on page 104 for additional information.

Titles

Capitals in Titles

Rule 24

A Rewrite each title, using capitals where they are needed. Remember to underline titles of books, movies, and television programs.

1. the little prince _____

2. around the world in eighty days _____

3. the witch of blackbird pond _____

4. where the red fern grows _____

5. the incredible journey _____

6. the wind in the willows _____

7. the girl who loved wild horses _____

8. my friend flicka _____

9. the pioneers go west _____

10. the wizard of oz _____

B Write these titles. Be sure to use capitals correctly.

your favorite book _____

your favorite movie _____

your favorite TV show _____

Name _____

Books, Movies, Songs, Stories

Rule 24

Use Rule 24 to decide whether each title should be underlined or placed in quotation marks. Rewrite each sentence using the correct punctuation.

1. My friends came over to watch the movie The Adventures of Robin Hood with me.

_____

_____

2. Dad and I both think Jurassic Park is the best book by Michael Crichton.

_____

_____

3. Our chorus sang both Over the Rainbow and Sunny Side of the Street at the concert.

_____

_____

4. Millie read the poem Casey at the Bat to the children.

_____

_____

5. Grandpa's favorite television show is Law and Order.

_____

_____

6. Andrea wrote a story called My Dog Pepper.

_____

_____

Name _____

Favorite Titles

Ask a friend or family member to answer the following questions. Write their answers. Be sure to underline or use quotation marks correctly.

The person I talked to is _____.

1. What is your favorite book?

_____

2. What is the best movie you have seen this year?

_____

3. What story did you like best when you were a child?

_____

4. What song do you most often sing or hum?

_____

5. What poem do you find most inspiring?

_____

6. Name a television program that you think is educational.

_____

7. What is your favorite magazine?

_____

Rule 25

Some words are easily confused. Take care to use the following words correctly:*

• can—may

Use *can* to tell that someone is able to do something.

*Carrie **can** play the piano.*

Use *may* to ask or give permission to do something.

***May** she play it at the party?*

• sit—set

Use *sit* to mean "stay seated."

*Mom **sits** on the edge of the bed to take off her shoes.*

Use *set* to mean "to put or place."

*She **sets** her shoes down in the closet every night.*

• lie—lay

Use *lie* to mean "to rest or recline."

***Lie** down and take a nap.*

Use *lay* to mean "to put or place."

***Lay** your books on the table.*

• good—well

Use *good* to describe nouns.

*That pie looks **good**.*

Use *well* to describe verbs.

*My mother bakes **well**.*

*See Notes to the Teacher on page 104 for additional information.

Word Usage

Name _____

Can or May?

A Use **can** or **may** to complete each sentence correctly.

1. _____ I go to Sandy's party?

2. Margaret _____ dance and sing.

3. John _____ make dinner without any help.

4. You _____ not bring your football to the party.

5. I _____ carry all three packages by myself.

6. Mother says my little sister _____ not cross the street by herself.

B Write a sentence using **can**.

_____

_____

C Write a sentence using **may**.

_____

_____

Well or Good?

A Use **well** or **good** to complete each sentence correctly.

1. That fried chicken sure smells _____.

2. I wish I could play basketball as _____ as Arturo.

3. Sharon writes very _____.

4. My car is running very _____.

5. Skipper is a very _____ dog.

6. I made a _____ grade on my Spanish test.

B Write a sentence using **well**.

_____

_____

C Write a sentence using **good**.

_____

_____

Name _____

Lie or Lay?

A Use **lie** or **lay** to complete each sentence correctly.

1. Mom asked Ben not to _____ his books on the floor.

2. Rosemary wants to _____ on the couch and rest for a little while.

3. The hens _____ eggs in their nests.

4. If you _____ the newspaper on the bench it will blow away.

5. We love to _____ on the grass and look at the clouds.

6. Please _____ the towels on the chair by the pool.

B Write a sentence using **lie**.

_____

_____

C Write a sentence using **lay**.

_____

_____

Notes to the Teacher

Rule 4, page 15

The rule states that the parts of a compound sentence are **usually** joined by conjunctions. A semicolon may also replace a comma and conjunction in a compound sentence.

Simple sentences: *He broke the window. It was an accident.*

Compound sentence: *He broke the window; it was an accident.*

Rule 8, page 31

A more complete way of stating this rule would be as follows: An **object pronoun** is used after an action verb or a preposition.

However, as prepositions are not addressed until the fifth-grade book in this series, the reference to prepositions was omitted. Here are some examples of an object pronoun following a preposition:

*One of **you** is the winner.*

*Both of **them** like to play baseball.*

Rule 16, page 63

The present tense endings *s* and *es* are used only with third person singular nouns and pronouns (*he, she, it, Grandma, Mr. Jones*, etc.). The distinction between first person and third person may need to be explained to non-native speakers.

Rule 21, page 83

You may also wish to teach this rule:

- In running text, a comma follows as well as precedes both the year and the state, province, or country.

The events of April 18, 1775, have long been celebrated in song and story.

The electrical storms in Flagstaff, Arizona, are no less than spectacular.

Rule 23, page 91

You may also wish to teach this rule:

- We usually use a comma to separate the quotation from the rest of the sentence.

"This is a good book," stated Tony.

Tony stated, "This is a good book."

Tony asked, "Is this a good book?"

"Is this a good book?" asked Tony.
(A question mark takes the place of the comma.)

Notes to the Teacher
(continued)

Rule 24, page 95

The rule states that the first word, the last word, and every important word in between should be capitalized. Words that are not capitalized are usually articles (*a, an, the*), short prepositions (*at, by, from, in, of, to*), and short conjunctions (*and, or, but*).

Rule 25, page 99

Well is often confused with **good**.

• **Good** is an adjective and **well** is *usually* an adverb.

> *She is a **good** musician.*
> *She plays both the piano and the guitar **well**.*

> *I received a **good** grade on the social studies test.*
> *All the time spent studying served me **well**.*

• Both **well** and **good** are correct in this instance.

> *"After all that food, I don't feel **well**," groaned Melvin.*
> *"I don't feel **good**, either," complained Marvin.*

• Although both **well** and **good** are correct here, the meaning in sentence two may be unclear.

> *You don't look **well**. (You look sick.)*
> *You don't look **good**. (It could be that you look sick,*
> *or it could be that your appearance isn't appealing.)*

Answer Key

Page 4

1. ? question
2. . statement
3. . command
4. ! exclamation OR . statement
5. ! exclamation
6. . statement
7. ? question
8. . command

Sentences will vary, but they should reflect the requested sentence types.

Page 5

Sentences will vary. Check for correct punctuation.

Page 6

Sentences will vary, but should go with statements.

Page 8

1. The whole team (cheered for their coach.)
2. I (feed my neighbor's cat.)
3. The hungry children (ate the leftover pizza)
4. Sally (mowed the lawn after school.)
5. Carlos (receives his allowance every Friday.)

Sentences will vary.

Page 9

Sentences will vary.

Page 10

Numbers 3, 4, 9, 11, 13, and 14 should be circled.

Page 12

1. My sister Amy **SS** gave me her old bike.
2. The large package **SS** was from Uncle Pete.
3. Several school bands **SS** marched in the parade.
4. George's pet dog **SS** caught the ball.
5. The frightened mouse **SS** ran behind the stove.
6. Everyone in the play **SS** did a good job.

Answers will vary.

Page 13

1. My brother Ted **SP** gave me his old skates.
2. The largest giraffe **SP** ate from the top of the tree.

Page 13 (continued)

3. Many teams **SP** played in the baseball league.
4. Angela's pet hamster **SP** escaped from its cage.
5. The frightened puppy **SP** hid under Bob's bed.
6. We all **SP** helped wash the dirty car.

Answers will vary.

Page 14

Our school's marching band performed the national anthem.

Sixteen wild mustangs galloped across the prairie.

The courageous fire fighters rescued me from the burning building.

My little baby brother cried when he lost his blanket.

Rhonda's nephew Ray mowed the grass all by himself.

Mrs. Hamilton and Mr. Peters organized the community softball game.

The little pink pig splashed in the mud and squealed.

The whole class went on the field trip.

A tired, old dog slept in the sunshine.

Two small green frogs jumped off a log and into the pond.

Page 16

Mrs. Clark has an interesting job. She is a veterinarian, (and) she works in a zoo. She gives the animals medicine when they are sick, (and) she operates on them sometimes. She can clean their teeth, (but) she has to call a dentist to take care of bad teeth. Do you think you would like this job, (or) would you hate it?

Sentences will vary.

Page 17

Numbers 1, 4, and 5 should be underlined. Numbers 2, 3, and 6 should be circled.

Sentences will vary. Check for correct simple and compound sentences.

Page 18

1. The children traded baseball cards, and then they talked about the players.
2. The immigrants crossed the ocean, and finally they reached a new land.
3. Do you want to go to the movies, or would you rather go to the soccer game?
4. Eric wanted to go play ball with his friends, but he had to give the dog a bath first.

Page 20

bake   long   (Sally)
(school)   (bicycle)   fuzzy
(father)   speak   (park)
curly   (book)   rough
(carpenter)   (basket)   (feather)
write   (Jake)   (Marine World)
(hospital)   reach   sleep
(church)   (friend)   (pickle)

person	place	thing
father	school	bicycle
carpenter	hospital	book
Jake	church	basket
friend	park	feather
Sally	Marine World	pickle

Page 21

1. Margo visited San Francisco, California.
2. Luis saw fireworks on the Fourth of July.
3. Columbus sailed across the Atlantic Ocean on the Santa Maria.
4. On August 14, Dr. Wang will begin working as a veterinarian at the San Diego Zoo.

Answers will vary.

Page 22

1. Dr. Green is my (dentist.)
2. We had Kentucky Fried Chicken when Rev. Williams came to (dinner.)
3. Juan Garcia and Maria Montoya are in Mr. Martin's (class.)
4. My (sister) and I stayed with Mr. and Mrs. Evans while our (parents) were in New York.
5. Carl's (birthday) is on Christmas (day,) but he celebrates it on December 26.

Page 24

cats	guⓍss	babies	banⓍage
cities	bⓍs	foxes	beⓍry
knives	vacⓍion	tⓍl	boxes
raⓍit	benches	cliffs	cherries

Sentences will vary.

Page 25

1. foxes
2. puppies
3. shelves
4. bushes
5. toys
6. cherries
7. guesses

Page 25 (continued)

8. stories
9. ditches
10. roofs

Sentences will vary. Check for correct spelling of plural nouns.

Page 26

1. penny, pennies
2. baby, babies
3. bus, buses
4. dress, dresses
5. glass, glasses
6. cherry, cherries

Sentences will vary. Check for correct spelling of plural nouns.

Page 28

1. men, women
2. mice, fish
3. oxen, geese
4. children, moose
5. feet, teeth
6. people, dice

Lists will vary.

Page 29

⭐ start ⭐

children	hero	cheese	gentlemen	wishes	men
dice	base	dress	socks	nose	donkeys
deer	shoes	rash	giants	size	libraries
kiss	people	mind	women	guest	dishes
grape	houses	thimble	babies	city	teeth
mess	mice	oxen	bees	gas	feet

⭐ finish ⭐

Page 30

1. feet
2. children
3. people
4. mice
5. teeth
6. geese
7. women
8. men

Answers will vary.

Page 32

1. She, him, them
2. They, it
3. He/She, them
4. We, it
5. they, it
6. He, it, us

Page 33
1. we
2. us
3. us
4. We

1. them
2. them
3. they
4. They

Sentences will vary.

Page 34
they OR them   he OR him
she OR her   it

Sentences will vary. Check for correct use of pronouns.

Page 36
1. I
2. me
3. I
4. I
5. me
6. me
7. I
8. me

Sentences will vary. Check for correct use of *I* and *me.*

Page 37
Numbers 1, 3, 5, 6, and 7 should be circled.
Sentences will vary. Check for correct use of *I* and *me.*

Page 38
Meg, Jane, and (me) went to the fair. Jane and (me) went on all the rides. Then we looked at the farm animals. Meg liked the baby pigs, but (me and Jane) thought the goats were cuter. Meg bought some corn on the cob for Jane and (I) to eat. We were still hungry, so Jane bought ice-cream cones for Meg and (I) After dark, Jane and (me) watched the amazing fireworks show.

Meg, Jane, and **I** went to the fair. Jane and **I** went on all the rides. Then we looked at the farm animals. Meg liked the baby pigs, but **Jane and I** thought the goats were cuter. Meg bought some corn on the cob for Jane and **me** to eat. We were still hungry, so Jane bought ice-cream cones for Meg and **me**. After dark, Jane and **I** watched the amazing fireworks show.

Concluding sentences will vary.

Page 40
1. girls'
2. dog's

Page 40 (continued)
3. mothers'
4. bunny's
5. workers'
6. boys'
7. band's
8. Kate's

Answers will vary. Check for correct use of apostrophes.

Page 41
1. bears'
2. giant's
3. troll's
4. pigs'
5. grandmother's
6. Cinderella's
7. witch's
8. emperor's

Page 42

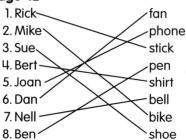

1. Rick's stick
2. Mike's bike
3. Sue's shoe
4. Bert's shirt
5. Joan's phone
6. Dan's fan
7. Nell's bell
8. Ben's pen

Page 44
1. his
2. their
3. her
4. Our
5. your
6. its
7. my
8. mine
Sentences will vary.

Page 45
1. their
2. its
3. her
4. his
5. their
6. her
7. your
8. our

Page 46
1. Serena found her hat in the closet.
2. I wrote my story about birds.
3. Randall and I whispered our secrets quietly.
4. Avery cut his finger with a pocketknife.
5. The cats ate their food from a bowl.
6. You played your saxophone beautifully.
7. The dog caught its frisbee in the air.

Page 48
My friend Tony and I (went) to the beach yesterday. We (climbed) on the rocks and (built) castles in the sand.

We (saw) interesting plants and animals in the tide pools. Tony (picked) up a crab, but he (yelled) and (dropped) it fast. The crab (pinched) his finger!

I (stood) too close to the waves. Tony (yelled), "(Look) out!" It (was) too late. I (was) (soaked.) Tony (laughed) so hard he (fell) down. I (will) be more careful next time.

Paragraphs will vary. Check that all verbs are circled.

Page 49
Answers will vary. Check for correct use of verbs.

Page 50

bee	horse	snake	eagle
buzz	gallop	slither	soar
sting	whinny	bask	scream
flit	canter	coil	dive

Answers will vary. Check for correct use of verbs.

Page 52
Possible answers:

paint	eat
talk	drink
hammer	sew
sing	play
dance	read
sweep	work
wink	walk
smile	sit
jump	stand

Page 53
1. was
2. became
3. tasted
4. is
5. were
6. am
7. is
8. looks

Sentences will vary. Check for correct use of linking verbs.

Page 54
1. (had) baked
2. (has been) reading
3. (are) flying
4. (had) won
5. (have) finished
6. (was) working

Sentences will vary. Check for correct use of helping verbs.

Page 56
1. play
2. are
3. paints
4. flies
5. lays
6. dance

Sentences will vary. Check for correct subject-verb agreement.

Page 57

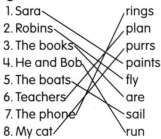

1. Sara
2. Robins
3. The books
4. He and Bob
5. The boats
6. Teachers
7. The phone
8. My cat

rings
plan
purrs
paints
fly
are
sail
run

Sentences will vary.

Page 58
1. are
2. is
3. are
4. has
5. have
6. are
7. has
8. is
9. have
10. has

Page 60
1. past
2. present
3. future
4. future
5. past
6. present
7. past
8. future
9. past
10. present

Page 61
Sentences will vary. Check for correct verb tenses.

Page 62

past	present	future
thought	sings	will send
removed	jokes	will buy
fell	speaks	will plant
climbed	enjoys	shall speak
lost	tastes	shall make

Page 64
1. bakes
2. hurries
3. tries
4. reaches
5. cries
6. rushes
7. fries
8. washes
9. mixes
10. passes
11. plays
12. buzzes

1. cries
2. passes
3. hurries
4. washes
5. plays
6. bakes

Page 65
1. played
2. jump
3. jogged
4. nibbled
5. tiptoe

Page 65 (continued)
6. will speak
7. raises
8. will visit

Sentences will vary. Check for correct verb tenses.

Page 66
1. past
2. past
3. past
4. present
5. past
6. present
7. past
8. past
9. present
10. past

1. flipped
2. agreed
3. carried
4. rowed
5. watched
6. tagged
7. dropped
8. tried
9. admired
10. hurried

Page 68

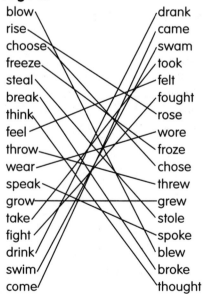

blow — blew
rise — rose
choose — chose
freeze — froze
steal — stole
break — broke
think — thought
feel — felt
throw — threw
wear — wore
speak — spoke
grow — grew
take — took
fight — fought
drink — drank
swim — swam
come — came

Page 69

1. sank
2. won
3. forgot
4. blew
5. found
6. wore
7. brought
8. slept
9. ate
10. drove

Page 70

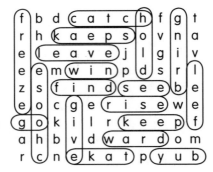

freeze, froze
catch, caught
hold, held
go, went
bring, brought
feel, felt
speak, spoke
leave, left
choose, chose
win, won
find, found
see, saw
give, gave
rise, rose
keep, kept
draw, drew
take, took
buy, bought

Page 72

Sentences will vary. Check for correct use of adjectives.

Page 73

Drawings will vary.

Page 74

soft	sour	delicious	purple	simple	strong
mushroom	jacket	building	resort	helicopter	busy
chapter	towel	ignite	sweet	tired	blue
nephew	introduce	pencil	small	sofa	paper
polish	respond	shoe	hard	enormous	cold
citizen	hobby	parachute	sleep	automobile	grouchy

Page 76

1. stronger
2. smartest
3. oldest
4. harder
5. warmer
6. kindest

Sentences will vary.

Page 77

1. The sun is bigger than the moon.
2. A lit candle is hotter than an ice cube.
3. A teddy bear is softer than a toy truck.
4. A giraffe is taller than a hippo.
5. A jet is faster than a bike.

Page 78

Answers will vary. Check for correct use of *er* and *est* endings.

Page 80

1. quietly
2. there
3. carefully
4. everywhere
5. patiently
6. nervously

Sentences will vary. Check for correct use of adverbs.

Page 81

1. carefully
2. everywhere
3. now
4. nearby
5. yesterday
6. quietly
7. quickly
8. early
9. home

Page 81 (continued)

how	when	where
carefully	now	everywhere
quietly	yesterday	nearby
quickly	early	home

Page 82

1. The little boy played (carefully) with the tiny puppy.
2. The kind clerk (cheerfully) helped the customer.
3. James worked (quickly) to finish his homework.
4. The sleepy bear growled (angrily.)
5. The large audience clapped (loudly.)
6. Mr. Yi plays the piano (often.)
7. Sarah whispered (quietly) to her best friend.

Sentences will vary. Check for correct use of adverbs.

Page 84

1. On April 9, 1942, my grandfather was inducted into the U.S. Army.
2. The Melvin family visited Vancouver, British Columbia, on their vacation.
3. The new school in Mesa, Arizona, will open on September 15, 2002.
4. The Empire State Building is located in New York, New York.
5. Emily Rogers moved from Nashville, Tennessee, to Seattle, Washington.

Page 85

Dear Beverly,

I am now a counselor at Camp Wildwood. It is a fabulous camp near Boise, Idaho. I started work on June 9, 2001. I am having lots of fun.

Your best friend,
Paulette

Dear Paulette,

Your job sounds wonderful. I will be traveling this summer. I am going to Paris, France, and London, England. I leave on July 6, 2001. I can't wait!

Yours truly,
Beverly

Page 86

Letters will vary. Check for correct use of commas.

Page 88

1. We went to the movies with Careen, Paul, and Maria.
2. Mrs. Clancy planted roses, tulips, zinnias, and carnations in her flower garden.
3. We ate sandwiches, potato chips, and cookies at the picnic.

Page 88 (continued)

4. Snakes, fish, and turtles all have scales.
5. Did you go to Disneyland, Magic Mountain, or Marine World on your vacation?
6. The children ran on the beach, waded in the water, and built sand castles.
7. Mosquitoes, crickets, and owls kept the campers awake most of the night.
8. Lightning flashed, thunder roared, and gusty winds blew during the storm.

Sentences will vary.

Page 89

Answers will vary. Check for correct use of commas.

Page 90

"Rudy, may..."
"No, Alex, you..."
"Well, why won't..."
"Because, Alex, the..."
"Gee, Rudy, I..."
"Okay, Alex, you...But"

Page 92

1. Maggie said, "I'll get us something to eat."
2. "Do you have any brothers?" asked Bill.
3. Beth shouted, "Keep away from that fire!"
4. "Why do I always have to take out the garbage?" complained Chris.
5. Willie said, "I want to be a veterinarian when I grow up."
6. "The game will start in a few minutes," announced the coach.

Sentences will vary. Check for correct use of quotation marks.

Page 93

1. "The class party starts at two o'clock," said Leonard.
2. "I saw an accident on the highway," Fran told us.
3. "Sam and Shirley are both in the play," mentioned Marcus.
4. "There will be a lunar eclipse tonight," our teacher explained.
5. "We have a science test tomorrow," Mr. Jennings reminded me.

Page 94

Answers and drawings will vary.

Page 96

1. The Little Prince
2. Around the World in Eighty Days
3. The Witch of Blackbird Pond

Page 96 (continued)
4. Where the Red Fern Grows
5. The Incredible Journey
6. The Wind in the Willows
7. The Girl Who Loved Wild Horses
8. My Friend Flicka
9. The Pioneers Go West
10. The Wizard of Oz

Answers will vary. Check for correct capitalization.

Page 97
1. My friends came over to watch the movie The Adventures of Robin Hood with me.
2. Dad and I both think Jurassic Park is the best book by Michael Crichton.
3. Our chorus sang both "Over the Rainbow" and "Sunny Side of the Street" at the concert.
4. Millie read the poem "Casey at the Bat" to the children.
5. Grandpa's favorite television show is Law and Order.
6. Andrea wrote a story called "My Dog Pepper."

Page 98
Answers will vary. Check for correct capitalization and punctuation of titles.

Page 100
1. May
2. can
3. can
4. may
5. can
6. may

Sentences will vary. Check for correct use of *may* and *can*.

Page 101
1. good
2. well
3. well
4. well
5. good
6. good

Sentences will vary. Check for correct use of *well* and *good*.

Page 102
1. lay
2. lie
3. lay
4. lay
5. lie
6. lay

Sentences will vary. Check for correct use of *lie* and *lay*.